What Others Say…

*The best way to describe Dr. Tammy Heflebower would be **transformational**. No one is immune to her incredible wisdom and no one leaves a meeting with her without first searching their soul and being resolute in changing their own behaviors and practices to reach higher levels of expertise.*
She truly inspires others in transformative ways.
Dr. Shelley Sweat, President & CEO, The Priddy Foundation

In my 50+ years in K-12 education with the vast majority of that time being directly involved in staff development and large group presentations, I have rarely encountered presenters or speakers in the league of Dr. Tammy Heflebower. She has a natural charisma and energy that are infectious. Perhaps, more important, she has the best technical presenting and speaking skills I have ever encountered. She has acquired such skill from focused study of the art and science of presenting and speaking, and has reached a level where she can and should tutor others who aspire to the same levels of expertise.

Robert J. Marzano
Cofounder and CAO of Marzano Research

What Others Say...

*I attended your "Powerful Presentations" workshop in Denver.
Your suggestions and tips made a huge difference and we had
our most positive feedback in 5 years! Thank you so much for
sharing your "tips of the trade".*
Sam Fritz, music teacher, Center Grove Public Schools

*I LOVED watching you work. You really brought your 'A' game!
I look forward to working with you in the future.*
   *Ramiro S. Reyes, Ed.D., Educational Administrator, Assessment &
      Accountability, Monterey County Office of Education*

*I appreciate your expertise and your input on the evaluation side
of things over a year ago, it helped us to move in the right
direction for sure. You probably do not hear it enough – but your
educational leadership is outstanding!!*
   *Melanie J. Mueller, Ed.D. Director of Research, Assessment and
      Evaluation, Papillion LaVista Community Schools*

Presenting Perfected: Planning & Preparing Your Message

Planning & Preparing Your Message

This is the first resource in the *Presenting Perfected* series:
Everyday solutions for
perfecting your presentations.

Dr. Tammy Heflebower

Dedication

To Mike, my incredible life partner who is my biggest

supporter and encourager. You helped me find my

message. Logan, and Nate—you ARE my messages to

the world! Now, go fine tune your own. Be bold. Be

brave. Be the best version of you, you can be. Thanks

for your love and guidance.

Table of Contents:

Introduction

It is January. I have been in my role as an author and trainer at a renowned research company for three months, and I've been asked to conduct my first keynote. The location--Montréal, where French is the primary language. Not only did I need to learn about a new educational system, but also their existing approach to my controversial topic of effective grading practices. I stood behind a podium—stiff and stern, I had memorized my keynote. I used limited inflection, my pacing was too fast, and I had to pause for the information to be interpreted and understood. The topic was a philosophical shift for the audience. There was no physical space for interactivity, so I aborted such infused experiences. Finally, it was over! I survived. They were polite, yet I knew it certainly was not a home run. It was maybe a dive into first base after a struggled at bat.

Afterward, I reflected. I learned. I revised. I committed to getting better, much better.

Selling your ideas is grueling! Whether it is being done to a board, a team, your staff, during a teleconference, or an informal gathering--conveying and selling a poignant, memorable message takes specific knowledge and skills. Do you know them? Do you have them? If you are interested in capitalizing your skills as a keynote speaker, CEO, sales manager, or anyone seeking to enhance your presentation and facilitation skills, this book series is for you!

This resource is the first in a series about fine tuning a memorable message. It culminates key learnings over the course of two decades of full-time public speaking, training and speaking engagements both nationally and internationally. These engagements were presented to a myriad of audiences which include local, state, and national boards, CEOs, service clubs, administrators, parents, business constituents, and teachers. Each book exemplifies focus on a particular element of making a successful presentation, and the many derivatives of it. It begins with planning and progresses through reflection—from the appetizer to dessert, so-to-speak.

Throughout this specific resource you will learn about how to plan and prepare for a meaningful message. Chapter one describes important considerations and needs of adult learners. Thoughtful planning questions as well as an organizational quadrant helps novice and expert presenters reflect about the meaningfulness and purpose of the message itself. Chapter two embodies essential elements of content, training formats, group size characteristics, and considerations for planning short- and long-term work. I hope this series will assist you in your planning, preparation, delivery, professionalism, and

reflection. Go be great!

"Proper preparation and practice prevent

poor performance"

Bob Pike (1994, p. 9).

Part I: Preparing an Effective Message

The needs of adult learners

Adult learners are different. At best, they can be interested, inspiring, and enthusiastic or at worst bored, jaded, and disrespectful. How an audience responds is related directly to you and the message you are conveying. In most instances, adults want to contribute and have their knowledge honored and respected. There are defining features of virtually all adult learning theories (Kolb, 1984;

Schon, 1993 & 1988; Dunst & Trivette, 2012; Knowles et al., 2012). Summarizing what the various authors espouse, leads to four key components of an effective message. It must be:

1. Relevant

2. Practical

3. Active

4. Positive

Thinking of these (RPAP) while crafting your message will ensure you meet the needs of adult learners. Below, each is detailed.

1. **Relevant:** Adult learners are task- or problem-centered rather than simply topic-centered. They need to know why what you are training is important to them. What problem might this solve? How might this make their lives easier? The useful past experiences and insights adults possess, enable them to be skilled about what is

likely to work and what is not. Although they are more readily able to relate new facts to past experiences, clearly connecting relevancy helps adult learners "buy in" to your message. If it is not relevant to their needs, they are not interested.

2. **Practical:** Adult learners consider immediate usefulness of the information. They are more impatient in the pursuit of learning, and they tend to be intolerant unless useful connections between your message and their practical problems can be applied. Adults bring their own experiences and knowledge into the training; they appreciate having their talents and information recognized and used during a teaching situation. Simply put, adults like learning that provides them with practical activities that build on their prior skills and knowledge.

3. **Active:** Adults want experiential learning. Adult students are mature people and prefer to be treated as such. They learn best in a self-governing, participatory, and collaborative environment. They need to be actively involved in determining how and what they learn; they need active rather than passive learning experiences. Adults are self-reliant learners and prefer to work a bit more at their own pace.

4. **Positive:** Matured learners appreciate appropriate humor and elements of entertainment infused into the learning environment. Adults are more intrinsically motivated; they are enthused by internal incentives and curiosity, rather than external rewards. Adult learners are sometimes fatigued when they attend trainings, so they appreciate any teaching approaches that add interest and a sense of liveliness. Use a variety of methods,

audiovisual aids, and a change of pace-- anything that

makes the learning process easier.

The following Table 1 and corresponding questions assist in

planning your message. It should guide your initial planning

for each of the features.

Adult Learning Features	Planning Questions for Consideration
Relevant	• How will your message meet the needs of the audience? • Why would they want to know or learn it? • What's in it for them? • What problem will this solve? • How might your content and processes make their lives easier? • How will you define or suggest specific skills? • What defines proficiency within skill acquisition? How will they reflect upon it?
Practical	• How will you recognize the existing talents and needs of the group? • Will you provide print or online resources for review and use? • Will there be time for participants to apply the information during the session? • Will there be time for feedback to refine skills?

Active	• How will you use your training space for active involvement? • Will you be able to modify any activity for 30-50 more or fewer participants? • Will you need materials to increase participation (handout, cards for sorting, sticky notes, markers, highlighters...)? • Will there be specific groupings you will use throughout the training? If so, what are they (dyads, triads, small table groups, around the room discussion partners)?
Positive	• How might you use appropriate humor to set a tone of fun? • What might be a positive quote, picture, or video to instigate a mindset for learning? • How will you monitor your own verbal and nonverbal behaviors to ensure they are portrayed as positive in nature?

Using these components and considering the planning

questions will assist you in creating a thoughtful message.

A great application is to use Table 1 immediately to plan something you are about to present. Color code each component on various colored sticky notes. During your planning phase, place responses to the questions on the corresponding colored stickies. This will denote answers to the various needs of adult learners. If you find you are missing a color, or you are too heavy in another, adjust accordingly.

In addition to the initial planning questions, Dunst & Trivette (2012) found that using different combinations of adult learning methods resulted in increased adult learner outcomes. Stated differently, when adult learners are more actively involved in the learning process, larger effects on knowledge, skills, attitudes and self-efficacy are noted. (p. 146). Think about learning a new skill—maybe a dance move or yoga pose. Initially, you learn the basic movement. You break down each smaller movement, then try it. As you

18

practice, you obtain feedback (maybe in a mirror, or from a trusted partner). You then add on more complex moves and add that to the skill(s) you just practiced. This pattern of new information, practice, and feedback helps you learn the skill incrementally. This experiential application of learning increases retention.

Time usage is also of the essence. In fact, smaller numbers of chunked content increased this effect, as did training settings over an accumulation of 20 total hours (Dunst & Trivette, 2009). Recall the dance move or yoga pose analogy. Each time the skill was broken into its component parts (chunked), then practiced, your brain was creating neural networks for learning that part of the dance move or yoga pose. Doing these small chunks repeatedly with settling time for the brain in between, increases the permanence of the skill. When planning the most effective use of training time, think smaller increments interspersed with practice.

In summary, adult learners approach learning in unique ways. They are more self-guided in their learning. They require learning "to make sense", and refrain from learning activities that are simply about compliance. Because adult learners typically have more life experiences, when they are confronted with new knowledge or an experience, adult learners construe new meaning based on their life experiences and are more motivated to implement it into practice.

Content Knowledge

As you plan, you will need to know and provide critical components of the information. This often involves defining key terms and concepts, as well as providing context and/or relevant background information. Read.

Listen. Learn. Explore the topic in depth. You must be the person in the room who has studied the topic the most. It may not mean that you know everything there is to know, yet it will be blatantly obvious to your audience if you lack content expertise. They have come to hear you teach them. You best know it well.

Another way to exemplify your content knowledge is to know experts and resources for whom and about which to credit and provide as examples. It helps to not only know others in the field who write about the topic at hand, but also offer tools to support the implementation of shared concepts or practices within your message. Consider using direct quotes, pictures or examples of successful implementation.

It is also important to ensure accuracy of the concepts. One way to do so is to support the current learning with research, when applicable. Use applied research and empirical evidence for substantiation. Meaning, use excerpts which answered a question or obtained information through real world observations. Another way to augment accuracy is to provide real-life examples of research into action. When you can share examples of real people implementing your suggested ideas, your credibility is strengthened. Consider personalizing the information to the location and the audience, strengthening concepts with personal or location specific examples and stories.

Additionally, you might decide to use the age-old, six questions filter to guide your content planning: Who? What? Where? When? Why? How? Explain your motivation to engage in a specific topic. Who needs to know? What is the idea? Where will this work? When might you use it? Why is this important? How might you do this? Answering these questions will help you think about the clarity and comprehensiveness of your message. It may also surface the cost–benefit analysis of resources like essential personnel, system readiness, and possible unknowns. Thinking through your message in this manner will also assist in anticipating possible questions from your audience.

Consider some form of quality message design. A format that helps you think thoughtfully about your topic might include the following:

- Identify the purpose and outcomes of the presentation clearly and at early stages.
- Develop key ideas early.
- Use and organize appropriate materials to support your message.
- Use meaningful, purposeful, and engaging activities and interactive learning strategies.
- Check for audience understanding and input on a regular basis; provide a means for adults to ask questions in a public and/or private manner.

- Allow time for application and reflection.
- Provide adequate closure and effective summary.

Applying these suggestions helps you design a learning experience that has a natural flow, and accounts for how our brains often absorb, sort, and apply information (Brookfield, 2006).

Key Point Requirements

Audiences have some similar, basic needs. One is to be respected as adult learners—much like mentioned previously. They come with knowledge and experiences that should be drawn upon and cultivated. What will you do or say to honor that? Consider surfacing what your audience brings to the table early on during your introduction to the topic. Honoring your audience early pays dividends later.

Although audiences have comparable needs, they also have some distinct differences. Some presenters will consider using a variety of products and/or processes for ascertaining the differences about how adults learn and consider information. You may have experienced these yourself. Some might include, but are not limited to:

- o True Colors (Adamo, J., (2014)
- o Strengthsfinder (Rath, T., 2001)
- o Emergenetics (Browning, G., 2006)
- o Compass Points (School Reform Initiative, Horan, S., 2007)

Although these types of categorizations all have unique distinctions, and they can be great teambuilding activities, I will opt for a detailed construct more specific to *training* adult learners.

Four Types of Audience Members

There are four types of unique audience members for whom you should consider (Weller, S., & Hermann International, www.hbdi.com). The first is more logical and methodical. They need the facts, the numbers, the data. They require you to answer the question, why? The second important audience type includes the creative and imaginative ones. They appreciate the pictures, metaphors, and seeing the big picture. They thrive knowing how things connect and ways in which to visualize it. The third type is that of more relational and emotional listeners. They appreciate your stories, and a chance to interact with others about the topic. The fourth is the practical and relevant group. Most adults appreciate this, as we mentioned previously, yet some audience members thrive in this area of application, examples, and details. As you read more about the distinct audiences in Figure 1, consider which bullets are most indicative of you, as an adult learner. Interestingly, that is the very type you will often plan for first, and amplify naturally when conveying your message. You may notice you have some needs in all areas of the quadrant, yet one type is often most predominant. Pay close attention to the words and phrases that describe that audience type. Plan accordingly. Closely consider the category diagonally from your strength area, as it consists of characteristics more opposite you. It is the one you most often overlook or even forego when you get pressed for time. Consequently, paying particular attention that each quadrant need is addressed helps enhance your message for all types of audience members. In fact, using the planning quadrant, depicted in the following Figure 1, you will augment your preparation (and later, your delivery) of an effective message.

Figure 1: Four Distinct Audience Members

Four Distinct Audience Members	
Logical & Methodical • Mathematical • Statistical • Example-focused • Problem solver • Technical • Factual • Performance-based • Achievement-oriented **Phases to connect:** *"The facts are..."* *"Research from ___ conclude"* *"According to experts..."*	**Creative & Imaginative** • Visual • Pictorial • Metaphorical • Possibilities-oriented • Curious & Playful • Risk-takers & Entrepreneurial • Big-picture-focused **Phrases to connect:** *"Imagine this..."* *"Consider these options..."* *"What if..."*
Relevant & Practical • Applicable • Example-focused • Sequential and Detail-oriented • Realistic • Doer • Information user • Reliable & Predictable • Cautious **Phrases to connect:** *"Here's how this could work..."* *"You could use this to..."* *"A simple solution might be..."*	**Relational & Emotional** • Storyteller • Musical • Teacher • Expressive • Reflective • People person • Compassionate & Sensitive • Talker & Connector **Phrases to connect:** *"Have you ever felt like..."* *"Others might feel..."* *"Once this happened to me..."*

Modified from Weller, S., & Hermann International www.hbdi.com

These variations in audience members and corresponding suggested phrases will help you in planning an all-inclusive message.

Not only are there various types of learners within an adult audience, there is also a suggested process for addressing each of the various learner types throughout a presentation. First, begin with the facts and figures; meet the needs of the logical thinkers. Capturing them early on will help them listen (and even tolerate) later messages and experiences. Once this group knows what you are discussing works, they will listen. Yet, do not overdo this, or you will alienate the other audience types. One or two key facts, figures, or charts will likely suffice. Next, consider the relational and emotional participants. Create your message with the people involved. Who will be affected? Where can you accentuate compassion throughout a story or a quote? Connect the *people* to the topic. After that, consider moving toward the creative thinkers. Here is a great place to share a metaphor to model possibilities. Use some creativity by involving the group in a visual depiction. Then, follow with practical examples of others who have tried or experienced the topic first hand, to reach your practical and relevant members. It is important to note that this is not the *only* way to approach the group through the lens of audience types. You may find a particular group is primarily comprised of only a couple of the quadrant areas. By all means, appeal to the masses, first. Yet, if you are new to this idea, using the following planning cycle in Figure 2 may prove beneficial.

Figure 2: Audience Planning Cycle

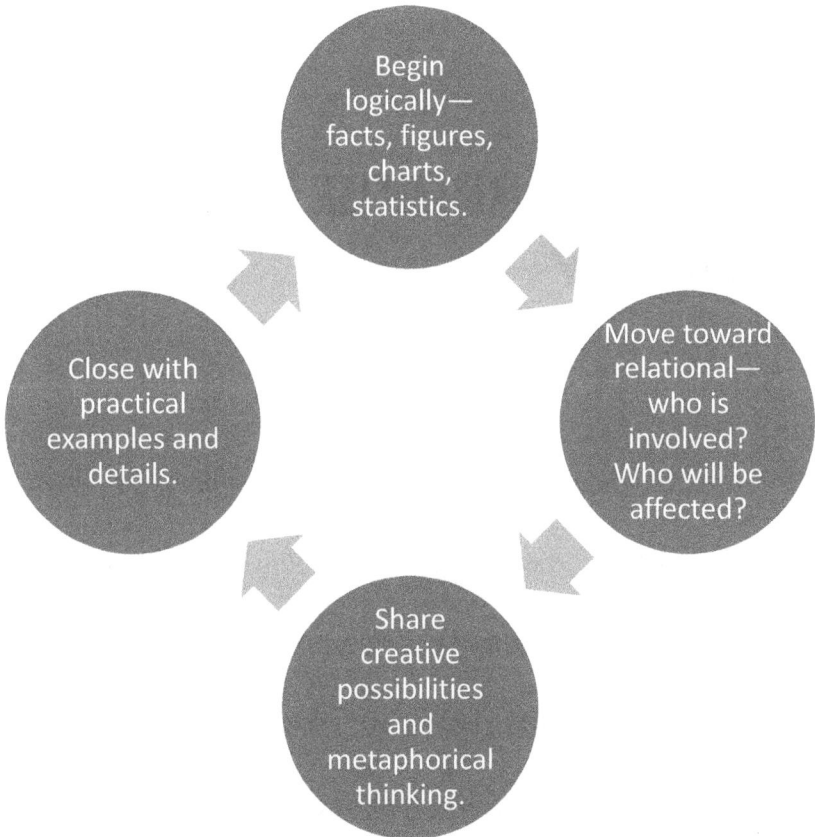

"Because ultimately presentations are

about the audience, not the speaker."

Akash Karia, (2015, p. 23)

Part II: Planning the Delivery

Audience Size Matters

Audience size is an important consideration. In fact, the size of the audience will invariably dictate the type of energy in the room, the types of activities possible for interaction, as well as the way in which a presenter will pace the content and delivery. For example, seasoned speakers often concur that a group of less than 20, is one of the most difficult with whom to work. The overall energy in this group is far less. Everyone has to participate, and it is more difficult to get the sound of mass voices into the room. As one of my colleagues once said, "In a small group, everyone has to get the intended humor. Yet in a larger audience, just over half can respond to the humor and it will feel as if the entire group does" (Williams, K., 2015). Comparatively, with large groups (51+) there is a natural energy — almost a buzz. Although it takes longer to conduct active participation, the sound resembles nearly a competition for air time. Think of it like when you go dining at a restaurant or shopping at a retail store. Listen carefully. There is music playing. For the masses, silence feels awkward and unnerving. In fact, there is a certain type of music, number of beats per minute, and volume level known to create an actual "state" of attention in the brain (Feinstein, 2006). Discussion of music use will be shared in a later volume about message delivery. In short, sound matters. Music and voices create energy in the room. You want, and need, them both.

Use following Table 2 to consider the similarities and differences among various audience sizes. In so doing, think about your group size preference. Does your topic work best when presented to a specific size of audience?

Table 2. Audience Size Matters Planning

Audience Size	Energy	Activities	Pacing
Less than 20			
20–50			
51–100			
101–200			
Over 200			

Below is a completed Table 3 to reference in comparison. This table details the features seasoned presenters might suggest.

Table 3: Audience Size Completed

Size	Energy	Activities	Pacing
Less than 20	• Limited • A few can dramatically increase or decrease the energy in the room.	• Dyads and triads work best. • Vary more with using some whole group discussions. • Charts may be seen and used effectively.	• Monitor for changing up activities every 20 or so minutes. Small groups may be able to go a bit longer. • Microphones are optional, and may even feel awkward in this size of group.

Size	Energy	Activities	Pacing
20–50	• More energy than in smaller groups, yet a bit more limited overall.	• Continue with smaller group sizes (2-4). • Easier for participants to network throughout the sessions. • Stirring the group and colleague cafés work well with this size of group. • Large group activities with all participants. • Charts still may work.	• Monitor for changing up activities every 20 or so minutes. • Microphones are encouraged. Even when people say they can hear, they can't easily. When in doubt, use a microphone and pace accordingly.

36

Size	Energy	Activities	Pacing
51– 100	• Solid and more consistent energy in the room than in smaller groups.	• Continue with smaller group sizes (2-4). • Movement is possible in most sized rooms. • Large group activities done with a model group of participants. • Teams of four work well. • Charts will be too small for this size of group. • Large screen and multiple screens may be necessary.	• Monitor for changing up activities every 20 or so minutes. • Microphones required. • Pacingwill slow a bit with mic use.

Size	Energy	Activities	Pacing
101–200	• Great energy. Laughter permeates the room.	• Movement is still possible as long as the room is capable of having some large spaces for such activities. • Large multiple (2) screens may be necessary.	• Monitor for changing up activities every 20 or so minutes. • Microphones are required. • Pacing will slow a bit more with mic use and room size.
Over 200	• Great energy. Laughter permeates the room.	• Audience movement is limited. Standing at or near seats may work. • Small dyads work for brief conversations. • Large multiple (3 +) screens may be necessary.	• Monitor for changing up activities every 25-30 or so minutes. • Microphones are required. • Pacing will slow extensively with mic use as room echoes.

Presentation Roles

Presentations occur in various formats. Sometimes a client requests a short presentation to inspire and overview a topic—a keynote. Other times, more in-depth training is needed. Yet other times, facilitating a group towards a consensus is warranted. There may even be times to do small group, or personalized coaching. Whatever the role, it is imperative to understand the differences and your presenter tendencies. Here, I describe the variations among these roles and responsibilities.

Keynotes

Keynotes are sessions that last typically from 45-90 minutes. They are focused on a single topic and are primarily intended to overview it and entertain. Keynotes are often delivered in large ballrooms where it is difficult to get much participant involvement. Keynoters need to be engaging in their presence and with their content. Not everyone can, nor wants, to keynote. In fact, some keynoters are lousy trainers and/or facilitators. In the same vain, some trainers and facilitators cannot effectively move into the keynoter position. DiResta (2018) suggested "The best speakers stay in their lane." This meaning that they know who they are and they capitalize their strengths of being either more of an entertainer or a content speaker. DiResta (2018) recommended that entertainers opt for the modes of keynoter or emcee. Rather, a trainer is more of an expert. Although certain types of presentations may feel more natural, it *is* possible to exchange lanes. Entertaining qualities will enhance trainings, and a topic focus will augment a keynote. However, the presenter must be very skilled. He or she must also know the strengths and limitations about each type of presentation, as well as how to adjust content and processes to fit the "lane" appropriately. This takes time, reflection, observation, and practice.

Training

Training is often completed within a few hours to full or multiple days with the same audience. Great trainers have specific content and processes to teach, and take on a bit more of a teacher role. They are versatile and must command an audience for longer periods of time. Trainers are more in command of the time spent on each component, types of activities used, resources necessary, and how the learning will be mastered and obtained. The goal of a training is for participants to acquire new information, techniques, and/or skills. A secondary goal is to transfer learning at a later time (International Association of Facilitators, 1999). A skilled trainer must be able to communicate the message effectively, as well as understand the audience's specific needs.

Facilitating

Facilitators help groups accomplish a common goal or set of goals about which they often could not accomplish alone. Facilitating an audience occurs during half to full or multiple-day processes, and it involves helping others face difficult, sometimes unobvious, issues with creativity and collaboration. Facilitators must master the art of questioning—knowing what types of questions to ask and ways to elicit open-ended responses that enable stronger collective dialogue, perspective analysis, and inclusiveness of the group. Although the end result is to achieve unanimous, win-win types of solutions, it is truly the journey that is skillfully facilitated.

Coaching

A coaching role is personalized, confidential, and somewhat complicated. A great coach recognizes the uniqueness of individuals and situations. Coaching conversations vary in pacing and styles (International Association of Facilitators, 1999). Similar to facilitation, coaching involves asking thoughtful questions with provided examples and direction as needed. A coaching situation is most often one-one or with a very small, trusting group of adults. The primary goal is to develop skills, reflect, and improve individual performance.

All roles are important to the teaching and learning process. None necessarily better. Yet the objectives and considerations are unique. A useful process for helping to identify the nature and characteristics of various delivery modes is in Table 4. Here, you will want to consider the various roles and what makes each role exclusive in the

training and delivery of content. To begin your thinking,

work through Table 4 on your own or with your training

partners. Draw upon your experiences to discern the

differences among the various roles and considerations.

Compare your thinking to the completed version in Table 5.

Table 4 Presenter Roles & Characteristics

Role	Description	Objectives	Unique Considerations
Keynoter			
Trainer			
Facilitator			
Coach			
Other			

A completed template might reveal other interesting ideas.

See some listed below in Table 5.

Table 5 Completed Presenter Roles and Characteristics

Role	Description	Objectives	Unique Considerations
Keynoter	• Short timeframes (45-90 minutes) • Requires clarity in message	• Keynoter directed • Limited content • Elements of entertainment • Practice or discussion is limited	• Short handout with key points • Slowed pacing • Carefully monitored stage movement
Trainer	• Breakout session, full-day to multiple days • More direct instruction interspersed with activities and applications	• Specific content and objectives provided by host • Learning blended with practice • Monitoring audience to direct pacing, respond to questions, add clarification	• Controls pacing • Pre-planned and created activities necessary • Handouts helpful

Role	Description	Objectives	Unique Considerations
Facilitator	• Varied timeframes full to multiple days • Often used during retreats • Consensus and collaboration imperative	• Goal for all to participate • Focused area of emphasis • Consider pathways and processes accomplish outcome(s) • Group often identifies the outcomes together	• Not in control of exact outcomes often emerge from the group • Requires flexibility and on-the-fly thinking • Skills needed in listening, redirecting, and tactfully handling unique adult behaviors • Handouts less necessary— often more charting or action planning templates involved

Role	Description	Objectives	Unique Considerations
Coach	• Short timeframes (30-45 minutes)	• "Coachee" focused • Supportive • Offer ideas as needed	• Questioning skills required • Listening and redirecting skills imperative

Planning Content Options

A skilled presenter knows the content well-enough to consider variations in what can be accomplished in certain time frames. Typical options are 90 minutes to multiple days—short-term to longer term alternatives. Variations in time will invariably affect the depth of understanding and the ease of implementation.

Shorter Term Considerations

What is your primary message? What is the soul of your information or idea? That, is what you share in your shortest time frame. Becky Blanton, (TEDGlobal 2009), underscored the importance of selecting a core message when she said, "Convey one strong idea. Take time to focus each idea you want to express, then pick the most compelling, the strongest idea" (http://bit.ly/244tM). That pared down, primary message should fit neatly into a 90-minute overview — a keynote in content. Done well, this type of message may actually be your "interview". In other words, this is a chance for the hiring agency to see what you present and how you present it within that timeframe. If they like it, they will sign on for more.

Longer Term Considerations

Signing on for more is the longer-term learning opportunities. Those may range from a few days to a few years. They require you to think about the primary, secondary and tertiary messages important to your topic. Remember what was mentioned previously about chunking out your topic. What chunks come first, second, and so on?

As you plan out multi-day presenting opportunities,

consider variations. These might include multiple overviews

with subgroups. Then, move into deeper training sessions

with cohorts (those learning together for a period of time),

interspersed with activities and application. Remember to

consider the various perspectives. Will you have a portion

of your message for the leadership team? Although similar,

it will have nuances about leading the work. Those actually

doing the work must deeply understand your messaging for

use over time. Build in follow-up and implementation

support to for this group to enhance the learning and

application of the message. Those may be done face-to-

face, via webinar, or even through phone consultation. As

you plan, ensure you consider a brief review of key content

prior to adding new information. This will help solidify

previous learning and provide the brain with the connected

neural networks for which to attach the new content.

Consider a 90-minute version, a ½ day version, a full day

version, and a 2-3-week version of the content. When you

have those typical formats, you can easily modify them to

fit other, unique presentation time frames. Use the

following table to outline your message points for the

variations in time.

Table 6: Time frames and Message Points 1

Time Frame	Key Message Points
90-minute overview	
½ day (4 hours)	
Full day (7 hours)	
Multi-day (20+ hours)	

50

Plan for New and Existing Staff

Remember to consider the needs of various experience levels when designing your presentation plans. Honoring those who may already have some experiences or different experiences from those who may be brand new to the company or entity is critical. First, this exemplifies that you know the differences. You also respect those who bring knowledge and experiences into the presentation setting. Finally, below are a few questions for consideration as you make your shorter- and longer-term plans:

- Who is new within the past year? How might their needs be different than veteran staff regarding your message?

- What do all groups need to hear and learn?

- How might you vary activities for the differences in experiences?

- How will you find out who is in the room? Will you do that ahead of time or during the introduction to the day?

Plan carefully for the diverse audience members within your training. Be certain to address those needs throughout both short and long-term proposals.

Throughout this section, I highlighted essential planning elements regarding content knowledge, training formats, group size characteristics, considerations for planning short- and long-term work, as well as considerations for various audience member experiences. Preparing your content and processes thoughtfully is an important first step in successfully fine tuning your message. The following book in the presentation perfected series details the significance of the message delivery.

Conclusion:

The suggestions in this book are that, suggestions. Pronouncing that every strategy offered will work in every situation is an overgeneralization. As Brookfield (1995) warned, "Issues in understanding adult learning despite the plethora of journals, books and research conferences devoted to adult learning across the world, we are very far from a universal understanding of adult learning (p. 2) http://nlu.nl.edu/ace/Resources/Documents/AdultLearning.html (1 of 11) [6/14/02 10:37:38 AM].

Despite this warning, the ideas shared, work! Experience with thousands of adult learners for multiple decades served as the premise for the advice and suggestions offered in this resource. You've got this! Go forth and fine tune the planning and preparation your message.

References:

Adamo, J., (2014). *Full spectrum success: living and leading in true color.* info@LiveInTrueColor.com.

Allen, R., (2008). Train smart: (2nd ed.). Thousand Oaks, CA: Corwin Press.

S. Brookfield: Adult Learning: http://nlu.nl.edu/ace/Resources/Documents/AdultLearning.html (1 of 11) [6/14/02 10:37:38 AM]

Browning, G., (2006). *Tap into the new science of success emergenetics.* New York, NY: HarperCollins.

Karia, A., (2012). *How to deliver a great TED talk.* Akash Karia. Kearsley.

Karia, A., (2015). *How to design TED worthy presentation slides.* Kearsley.

Dunst, C. J., & Trivette, C. M., (2009). Let's be PALS: An evidence-based approach to professional development. *Infants & Young Children,* Vol. 22, No. 3, 164-176.

Dunst, C. J., & Trivette, C. M., (2012). Moderators of the effectiveness of adult learning and method practices. *Journal of Social Sciences, 8, 143-148.*

DiResta, D. (2018, April 7) Public speaking success secret: stay in your lane [blog post]. Retrieved from https://www.diresta.com/knockoutpresentationsblog/public-speaking-success-secret-stay-in-your-lane

DiResta, D., (2019). *Knockout presentations: how to deliver your message with power, punch, and pizzaz.* New York, NY: Morgan James Publishing.

Feinstein, S., (Ed.). (2006). *The Praeger handbook of learning and the brain* (vol. M-Z). Westport, CT: Praeger Publishers.

Horan, S. (2007). *Compass points: north, south, east, west: an exercise in understanding preferences in group work. School Reform Initiative: A community of learners.* www.schoolreforminitiative.org.

Hunter, D. (1994). *The art of facilitation.* San Francisco, CA: Jossey-Bates.

Knowles, M. S., (Ed.). (2012), *The adult learner.* New York, NY: Routledge.

Kolb, David A. 1984. *Experiential Learning: Experience as the Source of Learning and Development.* Englewood Cliffs, N.J: Prentice-Hall, Inc.

Kolb, D. A. (2014). *Experiential learning: Experience as the source of learning and development.* FT press.

Pappas, C. (May 9, 2013). The adult learning theory — Andragogy of Malcolm Knowles, https://elearningindustry.com/the-adult-learning-theory-andragogy-of-malcolm-knowles

Peterson, D., https://www.thoughtco.com/principles-for-the-teacher-of-adults-31638?print updated August 30, 2017

Pike, B. (1994). *Creative training techniques handbook.* Minneapolis, MN: Robert W. Pike

Rath, T., (2007) *Strengthsfinder 2.0 discover your cliftonstrengths*. New York, NY: Gallup Press.

Schon, D. *The reflective practitioner*. New York: Basic Books, 1983.

Schon, D. *Educating the reflective practitioner*. San Francisco: Jossey-Bass, 1988.

Tough, A. (1999). The Adult's Learning Projects. A Fresh Approach to Theory and Practice in Adult Learning, *American Journal of Educational Research 2015, Vol. 3 No. 9 1133-1137.*

Tuinjman (ed.) (1995). International Encyclopedia of Education. Oxford: Pergamon Press.

Wild, J. L. (Writer). (1999, January 14). *Thread #3: Teambuilding & Communication: Facilitation, Coaching, Mentoring, and Training: Understanding the Differences.* Live performance in Williamsburg.

Weller, S., & Hermann International www.hbdi.com
Wilkinson, M. (2004). *The secrets of facilitation.*

Zakhareuski, A. (accessed August 20, 2018), https://busyteacher.org/7273-teach-adults-15-secrets.html

Biography

Tammy Heflebower, Ed.D., is a highly sought-after presenter and consultant with vast experiences in urban, rural, and suburban communities throughout The United States, Australia, Canada, Denmark, Great Britain, and The Netherlands. Dr. Heflebower has served as an award-winning classroom teacher, building and district educational leader, regional professional development director, national and international trainer, and leadership consultant. Tammy was also an adjunct professor at several universities, and a prominent member and leader of numerous statewide and national organizations.

Dr. Heflebower was the vice president and then senior scholar at Marzano Research prior to becoming the CEO of her own company, !nspire Inc: Education and Business Solutions.

Dr. Heflebower widely published. She is an award-winning author and coauthor of over a dozen books and articles focusing on organizational and educational leadership and teambuilding. She also specializes in powerful presentation and facilitation techniques, and is sole author of the *Presenting Perfected* book series.

Tammy holds a bachelor of arts from Hastings College in Hastings, Nebraska, where she was honored as an *Outstanding Young Alumna* and the team of which she was a part, was inducted into the athletic hall of fame. She has a master of arts from the University of Nebraska–Omaha and an educational administrative endorsement from the University of Nebraska–Lincoln. She also earned a doctor of education in educational administration from the University of Nebraska–Lincoln.

Dr. Heflebower regularly works with business and educational entities on site, and she regularly presents at national and international conferences. She provides

keynote coaching, facilitation, presenter training, and one-

one coaching. Contact Dr. Heflebower from her website at:

www.inspirementor.com, by email at:

tammyheflebower@gmail.com and follow her on twitter

@tammyhef.

Acknowledgements

I want to thank all those wonderful teachers and presenters from whom I have learned. Kathy Woodward, Dave Rosenbaum, and Jan Watkins, you were teachers who made such a difference in my life! You taught me when you did not even realize it. A special thanks to Robert Marzano for giving me the platform to hone my craft and use my skills. You have mentored me and helped my see and use my gift of inspiration.

To all of my family and dear friends, thank you for your unending belief in me and your amazing support. A distinctive thanks for my friends and colleagues Jan Hoegh and Phil Warrick. You have served as life-long friends and teammates like no others! You drive me to be my best, everyday! Thanks to all who challenged me to live my dreams.

www.ingramcontent.com/pod-product-compliance
Lightning Source LLC
Chambersburg PA
CBHW032018190326
41520CB00007B/526